Backyard Animals
Ravens

Christine Webster

Weigl Publishers Inc.

Published by Weigl Publishers Inc.
350 5th Avenue, Suite 3304, PMB 6G
New York, NY 10118-0069
Website: www.weigl.com

Library of Congress Cataloging-in-Publication Data

Webster, Christine.
 Ravens / Christine Webster.
    p. cm. -- (Backyard animals)
 Includes index.
 ISBN 978-1-60596-082-1 (hard cover : alk. paper) -- ISBN 978-1-60596-083-8 (soft
cover : alk. paper)
 1. Ravens--Juvenile literature. I. Title.

QL696.P2367W43 2010
598.8'64--dc22

                                    2009004175

Printed in China
1 2 3 4 5 6 7 8 9 0 13 12 11 10 09

Editor Heather C. Hudak
Design Terry Paulhus

Photo Credits
Every reasonable effort has been made to trace ownership and to obtain
permission to reprint copyright material. The publishers would be pleased
to have any errors or omissions brought to their attention so that they may
be corrected in subsequent printings.

Weigl acknowledges Getty Images as its primary image supplier for this title.

Arizona Sonora Desert Museum, Photographed by Lisa M Brashear, 2005:
Page 7, bottom left; Christof Asbach: Page 7, top right; Lip Kee: Page 7, top left;
Ron Co -Tasmania: Page 7, bottom right

Contents

Meet the Raven

Ravens are glossy-black-colored birds. They have a long, slightly curved beak, a wedge-shaped tail, and strong feet. The feathers on their throat are long and shaggy.

Ravens easily **adapt** to new environments and climates. They live in many parts of the Northern Hemisphere. Ravens are found in North America's hot deserts, cold mountains, and **temperate** forests. They also live in Europe, Africa, and Asia. Ravens are part of many legends, folklore, and stories from these parts of the world.

Ravens are often found in small groups or pairs. In wintertime, they will gather in large groups. Often, this is done near food sources.

Ravens often can be seen rolling and somersaulting through the air. Sometimes, they fly upside down for about 0.62 miles (1 kilometer).

Some ravens can copy
the sound of a human voice.

All about Ravens

Raven is the name given to about 10 types of birds that belong to the crow family. Common ravens are the most familiar of these birds. They are the largest of all the songbirds, at about 22 to 27 inches (56 to 69 centimeters) long.

Common ravens are the largest all-black birds in the world. They have sharp eyesight and excellent hearing. These birds are very smart. In fact, they are thought to be some of the most **intelligent** birds. They can **imitate** many different sounds, including the human voice.

Common ravens weigh about 24 to 57 ounces (680 to 1,616 grams).

Where Ravens Live

Brown-necked Raven

- Lives in the eastern parts of North Africa and the Middle East

Thick-billed Raven

- Found in the mountains and high plateaus of Eritrea, Somalia, and Ethiopia

Chihuahuan Raven

- Found in Mexico and the southwestern United States

Forest Raven

- Lives in southeastern Australia and Tasmania

Raven History

Ravens have been on Earth for a long time. The earliest **fossils** of birds similar to ravens are millions of years old.

In the 18th century, scientist Carl Linnaeus described ravens in his book *Systema Naturae*. The book was used to classify living things. He called ravens by the name *Corvus Corax*. This name is still used today.

Over time, ravens have settled near humans. In some places, these birds are thought to be pests. Programs have been put in place to decrease their numbers. In other places, there are few ravens. In the early part of the 1900s, ravens nearly disappeared from the northeastern United States. These areas have programs to bring ravens back.

Common ravens can make 15 to 33 different sounds.

In nature, ravens live about 10 to 15 years. Ravens that are under the care of humans can live more than twice as long.

Raven Shelter

Ravens live in many types of **habitats**. They make their homes in thick forests, on prairies, and in deserts and canyons. Some ravens live along the sea coast. Others make their homes on farmers' fields, small towns, and busy cities.

Ravens like to build their nests in high areas. This can include cliffs, large poles, or tall buildings. Ravens first look for a platform to place their nest. Then, they begin building their nest out of sticks and twigs. The sticks and twigs are woven into a basket shape. Inside, ravens line the nest with layers of mud, fur, bark, grass, and paper.

Ravens can live in places that have cold weather. This is because their black feathers absorb heat.

Ravens are strong fliers.
They can hover in one place
or soar high in the air.

Raven Features

Raven bodies are made for flying and catching **prey**. They can live in many climates and parts of the world. They have many features to help them do these things.

SOUND
The raven's call is a deep croaking "rrronk" sound. The bird makes other sounds that are similar to knocks and a ringing bell.

BILL
A raven's bill is long and slightly hooked. The powerful bill can crack open seeds or pull apart tough **carrion**.

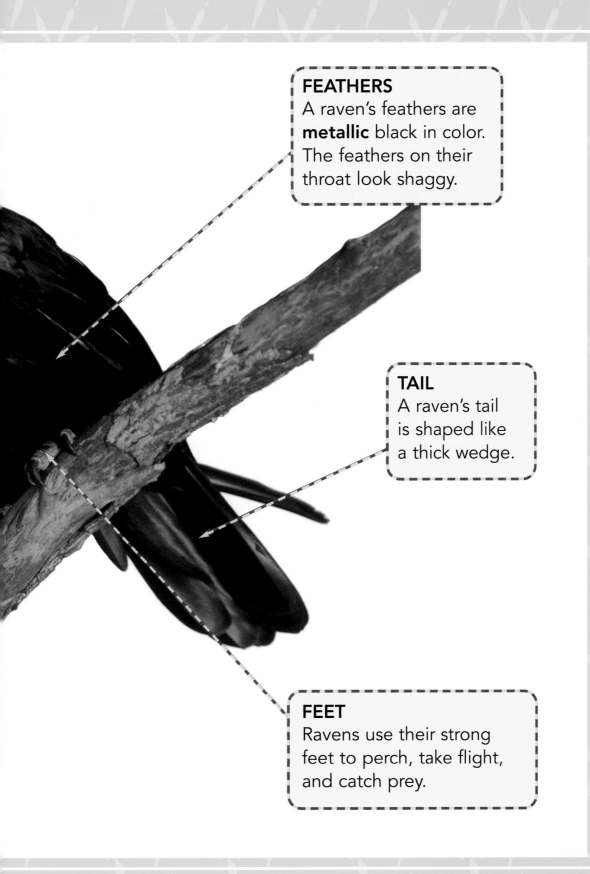

FEATHERS
A raven's feathers are **metallic** black in color. The feathers on their throat look shaggy.

TAIL
A raven's tail is shaped like a thick wedge.

FEET
Ravens use their strong feet to perch, take flight, and catch prey.

What Do Ravens Eat?

Ravens are **omnivorous**, but they mainly eat meat. They hunt small animals, such as mice, snakes, lizards, and birds. Ravens also eat eggs, bugs, grains, berries, fruit, and garbage. They usually find their food on the ground, but sometimes ravens will look for food in trees.

Ravens are **scavengers**. They fly overhead looking for carrion. When ravens spot a **carcass**, they land near it. Then, they hop forward or sideways to the carcass to eat it.

Sometimes, ravens work together to find food.

Before landing near carrion, ravens look for other birds, such as blue jays and crows. If these birds are at the site, then ravens know the area is safe from danger.

Raven Life Cycle

Ravens mate when they are between three and four years old. Once they choose a mate, ravens stay together for life. The female raven lays her eggs in a nest that is built on a bridge, cliff, tree, building, and large pole.

Eggs

A raven lays about three to seven eggs at a time. The eggs are a greenish blue with streaks and spots of brown. The male raven feeds the female while she keeps the eggs warm.

Babies

Baby ravens hatch after about 20 days. They have no feathers. They are sparsely covered in **down**. The male brings food to the nest for both mother and babies. After four to seven weeks, the babies will fly out of the nest. They stay close for a few more weeks. Then, they are ready to live on their own.

Both parents help feed the young. To feed their babies, the parents **regurgitate** their food and water from a pouch in their throat.

Adults

At night, ravens travel in flocks and **roost**. Before dawn, the group divides, as ravens search alone or in pairs for food. Ravens usually travel about 30 miles (48 km) a day in search of food.

Encountering Ravens

Ravens are a common sight in the skies around cities, towns, and in the country. Many birdwatchers enjoy sighting ravens. They like to hear their "cawing" and other sounds.

Some people think ravens are pests. They can harm farmers' crops, cause power failures by damaging power lines, and scatter garbage. Ravens have even pecked holes in airplane wings and stolen golf balls.

Sometimes, a raven may become injured. Babies may fall out of the nest, or an adult may fly into a window. If you find an injured raven, contact a local wildlife office. Place the raven in a cardboard box, and keep it in a safe, warm place.

Useful Websites

To learn more about ravens, check out **www.desertusa.com/mag99/ oct/papr/raven.html**.

Unlike many other types of birds, ravens do not migrate. This means they do not fly to warmer climates during the winter.

Myths and Legends

Different cultures have many legends, stories, and poems about ravens. Often, ravens take on the role of a thief, cheater, or a trickster in these tales. Many western cultures use the raven as a symbol of death, danger, and wisdom.

Some American Indian stories tell how the raven is the creator of Earth, the Moon, the Sun, and stars. Other tales claim that some animals, such as the raven, could act like humans. They were said to be spirit guides.

American Indians in Alaska believe the raven brings the daylight each day.

Owl and Raven

According to an Inuit legend, the raven was not always covered with black feathers. This is the story of how the raven changed color.

At one time, Owl and Raven were good friends. Raven made Owl a black-and-white dress. Then, Owl made Raven a pair of whale-bone boots. Owl also began to make a white dress for Raven. One day, Owl asked Raven to come for a dress fitting.

As Owl tried to work on the dress, Raven became restless. After a while, Owl became angry and shouted at Raven to stop moving around. However, Raven did not listen. Owl was very upset and tossed the blubber from a lamp on Raven. This turned the dress black. From that day on, Raven was black in color.

Frequently Asked Questions

What is the difference between a common raven and a crow?

Answer: Common ravens are almost twice as large as most crows. They grow to about 24 inches (61 centimeters) long, with a wingspan of about 4 feet (1.2 meters). Crows are only about 18 inches (46 cm) long. Ravens have long, shaggy feathers on their throat and a short, thick beak. Crows have smooth neck feathers and a long, thin beak. Ravens have a wedge-shaped tail, while crows have a fan-shaped tail.

Do male and female ravens look alike?

Answer: Both male and female ravens look the same. The only difference is their size. A male raven is slightly larger than a female.

Do ravens have predators?

Answer: Ravens have no known natural **predators**. Hawks, eagles, and owls, and coyotes may try to steal raven eggs, but they are often chased away by an adult raven.

Puzzler

See if you can answer these questions about ravens.

1. What do ravens eat?
2. How does a female eat while nesting?
3. How many sounds can ravens make?
4. How do ravens feed their young?
5. What roles do ravens usually take in legends?

Answers: 1. insects, carrion, plants, fruit, garbage 2. The male brings her food. 3. more than 30 4. They regurgitate their food. 5. tricksters, cheaters, and thieves

Find Out More

There are many more interesting things to learn about ravens and other birds. If you would like to learn more, look for these books at a library near you.

Bradley, James V. *Crows and Ravens*. Chelsea House, 2006.

Herkert, Barbara. *Birds in Your Backyard*. Reader's Digest, 2004.

Words to Know

adapt: to adjust to new conditions

carcass: the remains of an animal

carrion: dead animals

down: soft, sparse feathers

fossils: traces of an animal that are left behind in rocks

habitats: natural living places

imitate: to copy

intelligent: very smart

metallic: very shiny

omnivorous: to eat both plants and animals

predators: animals that hunt other animals for food

prey: an animal that is hunted for food

regurgitate: to bring food back into the mouth after it has been swallowed

roost: the place where birds rest at night

scavengers: animals that will eat foods they can find easily in their surroundings, especially dead animals

temperate: a place that has mild temperatures

Index